YOUR LORD
IS A
BLUE COLLAR
WORKER

YOUR LORD
IS A
BLUE COLLAR
WORKER

SeedSowers Publishing
Jacksonville, Florida

Library of Congress Cataloging-in-Publication Data

Edwards, Gene
  Your Lord is a Blue Collar Worker / Gene Edwards
  ISBN 0-940232-16-2
  1. Bible Fiction. I. Title.

SeedSowers Publishing
P.O. Box 3317
Jacksonville, FL 32206
800-228-2665
www.seedsowers.com

Dedication

Two of the poorest people I ever knew. A youth who labored hard for his dad, in the poorest county of all America, and left home at fifteen so there would be more food for the other siblings.

And to a woman who grew up as "poor white trash," who followed her parents in the cotton fields of Oklahoma, living in abandoned storm cellars.

And both later one day met The Blue Collar Worker.

To my dad and mom.

ALSO BY GENE EDWARDS

THE CHRONICLES OF HEAVEN
Christ before Creation
The Beginning
The Escape
The Birth
The Triumph
The Return

THE FIRST-CENTURY DIARIES
The Silas Diary
The Titus Diary
The Timothy Diary
The Priscilla Diary
The Gaius Diary

BOOKS ON INNER HEALING
A Tale of Three Kings
The Prisoner in the Third Cell
Letters to a Devastated Christian
Exquisite Agony
Dear Lillian

INTRODUCTION TO THE DEEPER CHRISTIAN LIFE
Living by the Highest Life
The Secret to the Christian Life
The Inward Journey

RADICAL BOOKS FOR RADICAL CHRISTIANS
Overlooked Christianity
Rethinking Elders
Climb the Highest Mountain
Revolution, The Story of the Early Church
How to Meet in Homes

CLASSICS
The Divine Romance
The Day I Was Crucified as Told by Jesus the Christ

Chapter
One

The young man, Menrod by name, had just turned twenty-one. For days he had hardly slept, for he was about to realize his life's dream. Today he would leave Nazareth, journey to Jerusalem, and there live in the temple for the next nine years.

Menrod would study to become a *scribe*. He could already picture himself in the splendid robes of a man in that profession.

There were three such men in Nazareth who had just turned twenty-one.

The second was Zordoc. For a long time Zordoc had also looked forward to reaching twenty-one. Today Zordoc would journey with Menrod to the Holy City, and there he would study in the temple to become a *priest*. His dreams were as great as, or greater than, Menrod's.

So it was that Menrod and Zordoc left Nazareth together and set out for Jerusalem.

Who was that third young man, also twenty-one? He was an apprentice to a woodworker, and held no ambition to study in the Holy City.

Menrod was wondering why their friend was not going with them. Menrod remembered, "After all, nine years ago I saw him speaking to the temple leaders. It was a day never to be forgotten. I never imagined he had so much insight, at age twelve."

"We will pass his house on the way out of town. What a ministry he could have if only he received *proper training*. Perhaps priest? A scribe? A Pharisee?" mused Zordoc. "On the other hand, none of those positions really fit him."

"That is true!" responded Menrod.

"The only other possibility is that he will live out his life *here in Nazareth,* working with his hands," agreed Zordoc.

"Unthinkable," murmured Menrod. "Let us visit him at Joseph's shop. He is probably there. Perhaps he will tell us what his plans might be."

Sure enough, the two young men sought out Joseph's carpenter shop. Finding it, they asked the whereabouts of their friend Jesus.

"I am sorry," said Joseph. "My son was looking forward to saying good-bye to both of you, but he was called away . . . to repair a damaged door."

"Will he come to Jerusalem?" asked Zordoc. "He is now twenty-one."

Mary interrupted. "I believe it is his

Father's will for Jesus to stay in Nazareth and learn Joseph's trade."

Joseph smiled, stifling a laugh.

The two men were obviously saddened to hear that Jesus would not be with them for the next nine years, yet were too excited about leaving to dwell on their disappointment.

Mary and Joseph bade the two young men God's speed as they turned to face their new life in Jerusalem.

"We have now left the *usual* life to join ourselves to the most exciting of lives," observed Menrod as the two men passed through the gates of Nazareth. "Still, what I cannot understand is why Jesus, with so much potential, chose to live out his days in Nazareth sawing wood. There is no merit in being an apprentice to a *day laborer*."

And so, we know exactly what Menrod and Zordoc were doing on that particular day.

It is now a proper question to ask: What was going on at that same time in other religions of the world?

Oh, and what was *God* doing that same day?

Chapter Two

On that very same day, over in Greece, the heathen priests of that land, dressed in elaborate costumes, carried out ornate rituals and sacrifices made to the heathen god Zeus.

Over on the isles of England, the Druids were offering up human sacrifices on convex stone altars in order to assuage their gods.

Far away in the mysterious East, a new religion was beginning to blossom. Hoping to please Buddha and to reach a state of nirvana, priests robed in white chanted for endless hours until their minds became mush.

But what was God doing that day?

God was not on his way to the Holy City. And he was not a priest, nor a scribe, nor a Pharisee, nor some other category of Jewish minister.

Still, the two men who left Nazareth and journeyed to Jerusalem were themselves certain *they* were doing God's perfect will. Certainly this was the way men *should* be trained to serve God.

Was that really God's way?

In every one of those religions and in all those breathtaking rituals, at the center of them all were trained *priests*.

That means these men were above the laity. And most certainly above the working class. Furthermore, these men were not seen just as good men; they were treated as special and exclusive.

Was the way of Menrod and Zordoc truly God's way? Trained priests?

These men would eventually become aloof and distant from other people, following in the footsteps of their predecessors.

Just where was the Lord while all this religious training was going on? And what would the Lord be doing for those next nine years, nine years in which Menrod and Zordoc would be properly trained to serve God?

Like Menrod and Zordoc, the Lord would also be in training for those very same years. Intense training. Also the right kind of training. You might say the training of Jesus Christ was the very best way of being trained.

For the next nine years *your Lord* would be a day laborer.

God himself reckoned that having his Son be a day laborer was truly the highest and best of all training.

The Lord himself, in training to be a manual laborer?

Yes! His "seminary classroom" would not be anything more than a carpenter's shop!

Chapter Three

Returning to Joseph's shop that same day, Jesus learned that he had missed saying good-bye to his two Jerusalem-bound friends, and he voiced his sincere regret.

Jesus lifted a three-legged stool onto the carpenter's table. "One leg is broken," he observed.

Joseph eyed the cracked wood carefully. "We will have to replace it."

It was on that same day that Jesus' apprenticeship as a carpenter *ended.* Circumstances decreed that on the following day Jesus would be a journeyman. This promotion occurred because, on that very evening, Joseph passed out of this realm to join himself to the Father of Jesus Christ in other realms.

Chapter
Four

If Menrod were alive in our modern era, he would be considered both a great Bible scholar and a great biblical translator.

Back in his day, Menrod quoted, word-for-word, vast pages of Scripture and then before the day closed he memorized even more.

That was not all. Menrod made copies of the Holy Scripture. The first thing he did every day was to test his reed pen by dipping it in ink and writing the word *Amelek* and then crossing it out.

Then, out loud, he said, "I am writing the Torah in the name of its sanctity and the name of God in its sanctity." He read the sentence he was about to copy and then wrote the sentence. When he came to the name of God, he said, "I am writing the name of God for the holiness of His name."

If Menrod made an error in writing God's name, he destroyed the sheet.

One day someone reverently asked Menrod a very complex theological question. He was very pleased with himself as he noticed that the layman's face lit up in awe at the wisdom found in Menrod's answer.

Menrod was well on his way to becoming a walking, living Bible as well as a Bible commentary. It showed in his stride and the new tone in his voice.

And Zordoc?

During this same time Zordoc was practicing the endless priestly rituals which he had to learn perfectly.

Zordoc was learning the Jewish calendar of seven special seasons within the twelve-month year. He could tell you what each of those seven seasons depicted. He could follow every phase of the moon, tell the meaning of every special week, every holy day, and exactly when those special days occurred, what those days stood for, and exactly how to observe each of those days and weeks.

Every day, without fail, Zordoc practiced these sacrificial rituals, learned when to raise his arms, when to chant, when to pray. He was also learning the exact details of how to offer the morning and evening sacrifices, on what occasions to offer a dove, a bullock, a sheep, a lamb. And not only was he being taught when, but how, to kill each of these animals.

Beyond that, Zordoc was learning about every type of grain, what that grain signified, how to cook each grain, and the specific grains and ingredients that went into a loaf of bread. Most of all, Zordoc was learning all about the different incenses and how to mix them properly. He was becoming a master of the spices, what each spice meant, exactly how to weigh each spice, how much of each ingredient to place in a blend of spices.

He was also learning subtle movements and pious gestures which he had observed the older priests doing.

As were all priests, Zordoc was a member of a certain priestly order. One particular year his order was placed in charge of the Passover festival. Zordoc was elated. He dreamed of the day he would become a full-fledged priest; and perhaps, just perhaps, the lot might one day fall to him to enter the Holy of Holies!

And what was the incarnate God doing during those passing years?

He was sawing lumber and getting splinters in his hands.

There was something else the Son of God was doing.

One particular year Jesus spent most of his time trying to please a man named Parnach, son of Rerari, who was the town's leading grump.

Parnach had asked Jesus to build a

cabinet. Almost every day since, Parnach had come into the shop, there to find fault with everything Jesus was doing concerning that cabinet. His demands escalated with each passing day.

Jesus took a deep breath and patiently complied with each new demand.

Tomorrow would be delivery day for the cabinet. Parnach arrived early. When he saw the finished cabinet he was incensed. The cabinet was nothing like what he had ordered, and the workmanship was shoddy. Parnach demanded to have the cabinet, yes, but he would pay for no more than the wood itself. Further, he announced that Jesus "should be happy to get that much."

At that moment Jesus heard a voice within. "Let Parnach have his way. It is enough that Parnach has to live with Parnach. And remember, my Son, I clothe the lilies of the field. I will meet your needs—and Mary's needs—of such things as food and raiment."

Then, just as Parnach was leaving, he turned and stormed at Jesus, "I am going into the marketplace today and tell the entire city that you are a worthless carpenter, not even worthy of that title. I will tell everyone to never do business with you . . . ever. Joseph was a far better carpenter than you will ever be!"

Such is the fate of the common working man.

Yes, Menrod, Zordoc *and* Jesus were all learning many things . . . some more important than others.

Chapter
Five

Very near to Nazareth there was a new city being built by the Romans. Word went out to the carpenters of Nazareth that the architect of this new city needed to hire all the carpenters in Nazareth. An agreement between the Roman architect and the carpenters guild was worked out. Over a dozen Jewish carpenters could be seen every morning walking to the city of Sepphoris to take up the task of building this gentile city.

A few weeks later, however, all the Jewish carpenters were suddenly dismissed. A slave owner, it seems, had underbid the carpenters guild.

That night Jesus faced the ominous reality of being the sole breadwinner in a home of six brothers and sisters and the trusting mother who bore him.

And he was out of work!

That same evening Jesus took a long walk among the lilies of the field while also taking note of the sparrows of the air.

And what of Menrod and Zordoc?

Shielded from the everyday realities and

33

woes of the ordinary class of people, the two men went about their insulated lives, unconsciously assuming that all people were as safe in their livelihood as they were.

(Nor could these devout men imagine that one day they would be caught up in the high drama of murdering a day laborer from their hometown of Nazareth.)

Chapter
Six

Does it really have any significance to your life that while on earth Jesus Christ came out of the working class?

Look all around you.

Over there is a brother in Christ who is a ditch digger. And over here a secretary, and there a bank teller. There also, an oil field roughneck, an auto mechanic, a bulldozer operator, and a bus driver.

Look around again. See, coming through the door is the waitress who just worked a double shift in an all-night cafe. She is a divorcee, with three children.

Also note the department store clerk, the house painter, and the ever-uncertain salesman. Do not forget that farmer over there who, in quiet desperation, is trying hard to survive a serious economic recession. And that oil field worker? He seriously injured his hand a few days ago. Today he found that his future of being a laboring man was very dim. Crippled oil field workers have no place in that field.

All these men and women know the seemingly unending crises of working people. Never forget that *the* day laborer also knows. He knows what it is to be a member of the working class.

Always remember, God worked for a living. He had splinters in his hands and calluses on his palms.

Be comforted in this and know: The room he worked in was unheated, brutally cold in the winter, and unbearably hot in the summer.

His tools often broke. It was required of him to purchase new ones, which he paid for out of his own pocket. This laborer struggled to make ends meet. He knew the face of the slow-paying customers and *never*-paying customers. Beyond that, there were those who he really wished would never walk into his shop—the endless talker, the gossip, the vulgar, and, of course, those who seemed to be the kin of Parnach, the ones who could not be satisfied . . . not even if God was their carpenter.

Just as you experience, unexpected expenses arose that pinched the family for months.

You do not work alone, nor is your labor unnoticed or unappreciated.

Sweat poured from his brow, just as it does from yours. Do you realize that this Carpenter also faced the *boredom* of the daily routine?

He came home every evening just as exhausted as you. And he was *still* tired when he

42

awoke the next morning.

Your Lord, the day laborer, held the very same mundane job year after year.

The Father, the eternal God, saw the best possible training, the best possible preparation, for God's Son was that of being a day laborer!

The eyes of the Father saw those daily struggles of a man who was making a living by the sweat of his brow as being far, far superior to the hallowed training taking place in Jerusalem's temple.

Or anywhere else.

Jesus' training as selected by the Father: The daily and ordinary grind of life . . .

God's choice for his Son.

Chapter
Seven

No one ever had to tell Jesus where he fell in the caste system of society.

He was at the bottom. Nor did he mind! After all, observe his earthly beginning. His first bed was a feeding trough located in a very smelly barn.

The *Father* chose that!

God chose that the creator of heaven and earth would be raised in the midst of the lowest class of people.

Some God!

Some value system.

God gave his Son a low-class family and a boring job.

Have you heard any recent stories about the signs and wonders spontaneously taking place among the Eskimos? Or the miracles taking place among the Bedouin tribes of Arabia? Or that revival sweeping New Guinea?

Do you not wish you worked in the midst of all that? After all, *there* is where the real excitement is. Nothing like that ever happens in your workplace, does it?

You get up in the morning, drive to work,

hear the same old questions and give the same old answers. Beat down by the daily grind, you return home each evening weary and sometimes a little discouraged.

Are you a secretary, incessantly typing documents which have nothing to do with God's work on earth?

Or is it that you make a living caring for people's lawns? You water the grass and mow it, knowing full well the grass will need mowing again in just a few days.

Do you have a basement-eye-view of yourself? Others are doing so many exciting things for God. But you? You are keeping house! You spend the day shopping, trying to find the cheapest price so you can save a few pennies.

Tomorrow you will spend the entire day holding your child because it has a cold or the colic. The highest thing you did today was to do laundry and make up a bed.

You gained twenty pounds having your baby. And all day long, all you do is change diapers and then change more diapers.

You are at home all alone, washing and ironing shirts. The task takes all day. Tomorrow your husband will wear one of those shirts, just *once*. Then it will be there to do all over again.

Thank God someone understands. He sees

the worth of such a day.

And you, sir, you pick up a wrench to repair a car you have absolutely no interest in. Your sole purpose in repairing that car is no greater than a means to put food on your table for your family.

You feel others are doing the things which really count. You would do well to reconsider that supposition. God thinks that ironing that shirt, changing that diaper or repairing that car is something extremely important. More important than living in a temple learning to serve God.

That is the way *God* saw it.

Chapter
Eight

Reaching for a saw, a chisel, a level—those tasks rank high in the value system of God. The day-to-day routine of making a living is precious to the One who decides what *is* precious.

When Jesus the Christ, the Son of God, measured that piece of wood, cleaned up the sawdust, pushed hard against the chisel . . . God the Father was making holy the *mundane*.

Your Lord sanctified the *ordinary*.

Your Savior, the King of all kings, lived ten hours a day, six days a week, doing nothing but the trivial. He lived in the routine, the unimportant. And in so doing he was sanctifying and making holy those trivial tasks of *your* life.

It was that Carpenter who lifted *your* daily tasks and made them into holy things. Jesus Christ made your working place *noble*. Your Lord made what you do each day a holy and divine act.

Jesus Christ did the same things you do; and the Godhead saw those menial labors of his, and *yours,* to be the very best, most marvelous occupation.

Your eight hours a day, his day in a small

hole-in-the-wall shop, both of them are better than the religious training of all the religions of the world.

Being a day laborer rose above all of them. When you change your child's dirty diaper, you have equaled the work of God!

Chapter
Nine

What you have done today is beautiful and holy—as holy as what God did in the drudgery of a carpenter's shop.

Every day you go to do your task, you sanctify the workplace where you serve.

You cause the business of changing diapers to become an act of righteousness.

Did you wash dishes today? Did you feed your children? Then you have fulfilled the ministry. You have performed one of the *great* acts of a Christian and paralleled the work of the Son of God.

After all, what did this Visitor from the other realm, this God who came from some other place...what did he do for the greater part of his life?

He did what you do!

Never forget: God the Father selected the occupation his Son would do while visiting here! What Jesus did, what you do, it is beautiful in the eyes of the Father.

In the workshop of life, this is where *his* preference lies.

Dear sister in Christ, wash those dishes,

change those diapers. Dear brother in Christ, reach for that greasy wrench, shovel that dirt.

Work out those figures on your computer, type those worthless documents . . . and know that your Lord, back there in Nazareth, made precious the boring things of life.

In the meantime, your presence in your workplace causes that place to be invaded by the temple of God—the *real* one.

Exactly where did you accomplish these wondrous things? You did them *in* Jesus Christ!

Chapter
Ten

Never forget who you are and what you are. What you are is as important in the upside-down value system of the Kingdom of God as being a carpenter was to God the Father.

When God chose for his Son to become a carpenter, the Father was telling you what his view of *your* occupation is. He was lending you his insight into what He considered valuable.

Vacuuming a rug, planting a tree, repairing that roof, all have become *acts of God.*

Jesus was in a hot, sweaty carpenter's shop, *and* in God.

And you?

You are in the tedium of life and at the same time you are *in* God. In the eye of a very special Carpenter you are in the same daily grind as he was in. And you are in Christ, as surely as Christ was in God in a carpenter's shop.

Your daily life, like his, is the highest of all callings.

His shop and your workplace win out over the edifice where religious workers are trained.

Chapter
Eleven

May it be that you see through the eyes of God and the eyes of his carpenter Son that every day you live, everything you do, is an act of holiness and the fulfilling of righteousness. The work you do today is as much an act of God as was the labor Jesus did when he repaired a bench in his carpenter shop.

May the Holy Spirit *convict you of your* righteousness!

May you never, never forget: God not only chose his Son to be born in a smelly old barn, but he also chose that this same Son be a day laborer.

And remember . . . it pleased God the Father for God the Son to be in the laboring class of people.

Never say that once long ago Jesus *was* a carpenter, Jesus *was* a day laborer.

When Jesus came to earth, he was God; but while on earth, he learned humanity! Jesus Christ, God incarnate, added to himself the experience of being a human. When your Lord returned to the throne, he did not lay aside his earthly experiences of being a man. All that he did, all that he was as a man, these are still part of him, *now*. Jesus Christ is still a man. He was—and is—a carpenter.

A carpenter sits on the throne of God. Even today he could do a good job building a chair! Your Lord did not *used to be* a carpenter. He *is* a carpenter and always will be. The One who sits enthroned is *still* a day laborer.

So, in every day you live, remember this: Your Lord *is* a blue collar worker !

An Audio Tape Available

Before the release of this book, Gene Edwards brought this message, which is now entitled Your Lord is a Blue Collar Worker.

The message he delivered that day was recorded. When listening to it, you can hear, and even feel, the audience's response. You may receive a free copy of this recording by writing:

SeedSowers
P.O. Box 3317
Jacksonville, FL 32206
1-800-228-2665
books@seedsowers.com

The Chronicles of Heaven
by
Gene Edwards

In *The Beginning* God creates the heavens and the earth. The crowning glory of creation, man and woman, live and move in both the visible world and the spiritual world.

Experience one of the greatest events of human history: *The Escape* of the Israelite people from Egypt. Watch the drama from the view of earthly participants and the view of angels in the heavens.

Experience the wonderful story of the incarnation, the Christmas story, seen from both realms. *The Birth* introduces the mystery of the Christian life for those who have never heard the story.

In *The Triumph* you will experience the Easter story as you never have before. Join angels as they comprehend the suffering and death of Jesus and the mystery of free will in light of God's Eternal Purpose.

The Door has moved to a hill on Patmos. What would John be allowed to see? *The Return* invites you to witness the finale of the stirring conclusion to *The Chronicles of Heaven.*

AN INTRODUCTION TO
THE DEEPER CHRISTIAN LIFE

In Three Volumes
by
Gene Edwards

Living by
the Highest Life

If you find yourself unsettled with Christianity as usual ... if you find yourself longing for a deeper experience of the Christian life ... *The Highest Life* is for you.

Did Jesus Christ live the Christian life merely by human effort? Or did Jesus understand living by the Spirit—his Father's Life in him?

Discover what it means to live a spiritual life while living on earth.

I.

The Secret to
the Christian Life

Read the Bible, pray, go to church, tithe ... is this what it means to live the Christian life? Is there more to living the Christian life than following a set of rules? How did Jesus live by the Spirit?

The Secret to the Christian Life reveals the one central secret to living out the Christian life. Nor does the book stop there ... it also gives *practical* ways to enhance your fellowship with the Lord.

II.

The Inward Journey

The Inward Journey is the companion volume to *The Secret to the Christian Life*. A beautiful story of a dying uncle explaining to his nephew, a new Christian, the ways and mysteries of the cross and of suffering. Of those who have a favorite Gene Edwards book, tens of thousands have selected *The Inward Journey* as that book.

III.

The Divine Romance

by
Gene Edwards

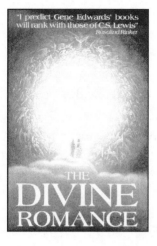

The Divine Romance is praised as one of the all-time literary achievements of the Protestant era. Breathtakingly beautiful, here is the odyssey of Christ's quest for His bride. *The Divine Romance* is the most captivating, heartwarming and inspirational romance, transcending space and time. In all of Christian literature there has never been a description of the crucifixion and resurrection which so rivals the one depicted in *The Divine Romance*.

Many readers have commented, "This book should come with a box of Kleenex." The description of the romance between Adam and Eve alone is one of the great love stories of all times.

Edwards' portrayal of the romance of Christ and his bride takes its place along side such classics as Dante's *The Divine Comedy* and Milton's *Paradise Lost*. Reading this literary masterpiece will alter your life forever.

One of the greatest Christian classics of all time.

The First-Century Diaries

by
Gene Edwards

IF YOU NEVER READ ANY OTHER BOOKS ON THE NEW TESTAMENT
. . . READ *THE FIRST-CENTURY DIARIES*!

Here is more than what you would learn
in seminary! The Diaries will revolutionize your
understanding of the New Testament, and, in turn will revolutionize
your life. The best part is, this set of diaries reads like a novel. Never
has learning the New Testament been so much fun.

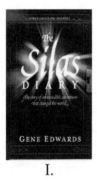

I.

The Silas Diary

This historical narrative parallels the book of Acts,
giving a first-person account of Paul's first journey.

The Silas Diary is your invitation to join Silas, Paul,
and their companions on a journey fraught with danger and
adventure - a journey that changed the history of the world.
Learn with the first-century Christians what freedom in
Christ really means.

II.

The Titus Diary

This compelling narrative continues the events of the
Book of Acts. *The Titus Diary* is a firsthand account of
Paul's second journey as told by Titus.

Join this journey as Paul sets out once more-this time
with Silas, Timothy, and Luke-and learn of the founding of
the churches in Philippi, Thessalonica, Corinth, and Ephesus.
Look on as Paul meets Aquila and Priscilla and quickly gains
an appreciation of their passion for the Lord and his church.

The First-Century Diaries

III.

The Timothy Diary

In *The Timothy Diary* Paul's young Christian companion Timothy gives a firsthand account of Paul's third journey.

This journey is quite different from Paul's others. It is the fulfillment of Paul's dream, for in Ephesus Paul trains a handful of young men to take his place after his death. Paul follows Christ's example in choosing and training disciples to spread the gospel and encourage the growth of the church.

IV.

The Priscilla Diary

Here are the stories of Paul's continued travels to the first-century churches narrated from the unique perspective of Priscilla, a vibrant first-century Christian woman!

See Paul writing his most personally revealing letter, his letter to the church in Corinth. Marvel at the truths Paul conveys to the church in Rome, a letter "of all that Paul considered central to the Christian life."

The Gaius Diary

Paul and Nero meet face to face in a moment of highest drama.

Paul is released, but soon is arrested again, and again faces Nero. The sentence is death. Just before his execution, all the men he trained arrived in Rome to be with him. *The Gaius Diary* gives life-changing insight into Paul's final letters. Colossians, Ephesians, Philemon, and Philippians come alive as you see in living color the background to these letters. Be there in April of 70 A.D. when Jerusalem is destroyed.

V.

For the first time ever in all church history, here is the entire first-century story from beginning to end.

THE NEW TESTAMENT

IN FIRST PERSON

The Story of My Life
as Told by Jesus Christ

Listen to Jesus, the Christ, tell His own story. . . in His own words. . . to you !

All four Gospels have been combined in one single, flowing narrative. And it is in the first person! The Story of My Life as Told by Jesus Christ is a complete and thorough account of the events of Christ's life. Now you can read all of the Lord's life in chronological order, without repetition of a single detail. Every sentence in the Gospels is included, plus times, dates and places.

Allow yourself to be immersed into the setting of the life and ministry of Christ. Follow His footsteps as He walked the earth with those He knew and loved, in one smooth, flowing, uninterrupted story.

The impact is so arresting you will feel that you are hearing the gospel story for the first time. And always, in first person, the Lord is speaking directly to you. Think of it as The Jesus Diary.

Acts in First Person

For the first time in history, you can read the Acts of the Apostles in first person . . . like a diary.

Listen to the men who lived during the exciting early years of the church. Experience the excitement and danger as these men travel to declare Jesus Christ. Every detail is included . . . such as dates and location.

Based on Tyndale's New Living Translation Bible, *Acts in First Person* is in readable, contemporary English. A wonderful study aid for all ages.

Books that Heal

Hundreds of thousands of Christians all over the world have received healing while reading these books.

Exquisite Agony
(formerly titled *Crucified by Christians*)
Gene Edwards

Here is healing for hurting and disillusioned Christians who have known the pain of betrayal at the hand of another believer.

This book has brought restoration to Christians all over the world who had lost all hope. Edwards takes you to a high place to see your pain and suffering from the viewpoint of the Lord.

Read this book and learn the *privilege of betrayal* and discover who the real author of your crucifixion is!

Letters to a Devastated Christian
Gene Edwards

The Christian landscape is covered with the remains of lives ruined at the hands of authoritarian movements. Some believers never recover. Others are the walking wounded.

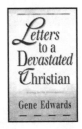

In *Letters to a Devastated Christian*, Edwards has written a series of letters to a brokenhearted Christian and points him to healing in Christ. This book is full of profound healing and hope.

The Prisoner in the Third Cell
Gene Edwards

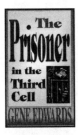

This is a book of comfort, told as an unforgettable drama, for those caught up in circumstances of life they do not understand.

In this dramatic story, John the Baptist, imprisoned by Herod and awaiting death, struggles to understand a Lord who did not live up to his expectations.

If you are a suffering Christian or know of one, this book will bring enormous comfort and insight into the ways of God.

A Tale of Three Kings
Gene Edwards

Myriads of Christians have experienced pain, loss and heartache at the hands of other believers. This compelling story offers comfort, healing and hope for these wounded ones. Probably more Christians have turned to *A Tale of Three Kings* for heal-

ing than to any other book for decades.

This simple, powerful, and beautiful story has been recommended by Christians throughout the world.

Library of Spiritual Classics

Jeanne Guyon wrote *Experiencing the Depths of Jesus Christ* around 1685. For over three hundred years, this book has led untold numbers of Christians to the riches of fellowship with Jesus Christ.

This little book on prayer will revolutionize your relationship with the Lord.

We have received thousands of calls and letters from Christians impacted by the writings contained in this book. The most prevalent comment is, "I can experience and know my Lord today in a real way."

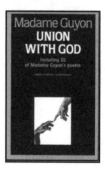

Union with God contains Jeanne Guyon's spiritual progression in the Lord. She reveals her desire to love only Jesus Christ, to live only for Him, and to suffer for Him. In her abandonment to her Lord, she acknowledges all things from the hand of her beloved.

Guyon reminds us that the Lord dwells within…and within is where we seek him…and there enjoy him in oneness.

You will marvel at Guyon's devotion to Jesus Christ, a devotion that she desired all believers to have towards the Lord.

We have included twenty-two of her poems that reveal a vast depth of love and understanding as to the ways of God. *Union with God* will point you to that place of infinite peace found only in Jesus Christ.

Fenelon lived during the period of Louis XIV in the 1600's. *The Seeking Heart* is an updated version of a series of spiritual letters Fenelon wrote to seekers of his time. Although written to individuals concerning a specific issue, the spiritual wisdom and counsel contained within these letters make them relevant for today. (The same is true concerning Paul's letters in the New Testament.)

After having read *The Seeking Heart*, you will come away moved by Fenelon's belief that God was in all things in his life. . . things fair and things unfair. He invites us to share this Christ-centered way of life.

Library of Spiritual Classics

The two best books in print in the English language on the *practical* aspects of the deeper Christian life are *Experiencing the Depths of Jesus Christ* and *The Spiritual Guide*. Both books appeared in the mid 1600's, yet neither author knew the other.

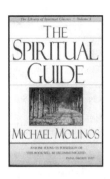

Molinos was tried and condemned and then sealed in a dungeon in Rome for writing this book. Afterwards, his books were burned. Nonetheless, *The Spiritual Guide* remains one of the great treasures of Christian history. Readers find this book to be transforming.

Next to *Experiencing the Depths of Jesus Christ*, this is the most *practical* book in print on the "how" of knowing Christ.

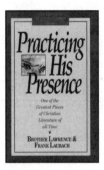

Be introduced to the joy of living constantly in the presence of the Lord.

Brother Lawrence experienced such joy while surrounded by kitchen pots and pans in the monastery to which he belonged. No job was too menial for him: "…to pick up a piece of straw was to do it unto the Lord."

First published in French in 1692, this little book has guided countless thirsty souls to a deeper and closer walk with God. SeedSowers publishes the easiest-to-read updated version of this timeless classic.

We have added excerpts of the letters of Frank Laubach's book, *Letters by a Modern Mystic*. Laubach lived as a missionary in the Philippines during the 1930's and practiced living in the Lord's presence.

SeedSowers Publishing House

P.O. Box 3317

Jacksonville, FL 32206

1-800-228-2665

www.seedsowers.com

SeedSowers
800-228-2665   (fax) 904-598-3456
www.seedsowers.com

REVOLUTIONARY BOOKS ON CHURCH LIFE

How to Meet In Homes (*Edwards*) 10.95
An Open Letter to House Church Leaders (*Edwards*) 4.00
When the Church Was Led Only by Laymen *(Edwards)* 4.00
Rethinking Elders (*Edwards*) 9.95
Revolution, The Story of the Early Church (*Edwards*) 10.95
The Silas Diary (*Edwards*) 9.99
The Titus Diary (*Edwards*) 8.99
The Timothy Diary (*Edwards*) 9.99
The Priscilla Diary (*Edwards*) 9.99
The Gaius Diary *(Edwards)* 10.99
Overlooked Christianity (*Edwards*) 14.95
Pagan Christianity *(Viola)* 13.95

AN INTRODUCTION TO THE DEEPER CHRISTIAN LIFE

Living by the Highest Life (*Edwards*) 10.99
The Secret to the Christian Life (*Edwards*) 8.99
The Inward Journey (*Edwards*) 8.99

CLASSICS ON THE DEEPER CHRISTIAN LIFE

Experiencing the Depths of Jesus Christ (*Guyon*) 9.95
Practicing His Presence (*Lawrence/Laubach*) 9.95
The Spiritual Guide (*Molinos*) 8.95
Union With God (*Guyon*) 8.95
The Seeking Heart (*Fenelon*) 9.95
Intimacy with Christ (*Guyon*) 10.95
Spiritual Torrents (*Guyon*) 10.95
The Ultimate Intention (*Fromke*) 10.00
One Hundred Days in the Secret Place *(Edwards)* 12.99

IN A CLASS BY ITSELF

The Divine Romance (*Edwards*) 11.99

NEW TESTAMENT

The Story of My Life as Told by Jesus Christ *(Four gospels blended)* 14.95
The Day I was Crucified as Told by Jesus the Christ 13.99
Acts in First Person *(Book of Acts)* 9.95

COMMENTARIES BY JEANNE GUYON

Genesis Commentary 10.95
Exodus Commentary 10.95
Leviticus - Numbers - Deuteronomy Commentaries 12.95
Judges Commentary 7.95
Job Commentary 10.95
Song of Songs *(Song of Solomon Commentary)* 9.95
Jeremiah Commentary 7.95
James - I John - Revelation Commentaries 12.95

THE CHRONICLES OF HEAVEN *(Edwards)*

Christ Before Creation 8.99
The Beginning 8.99
The Escape 8.99
The Birth 8.99
The Triumph 8.99
The Return 8.99

THE COLLECTED WORKS OF T. AUSTIN-SPARKS

The Centrality of Jesus Christ 19.95
The House of God 29.95
Ministry 29.95
Service 19.95
Spiritual Foundations 29.95
The Things of the Spirit 10.95
Prayer 14.95
The On-High Calling 10.95
Rivers of Living Water 8.95
The Power of His Resurrection 8.95

COMFORT AND HEALING

A Tale of Three Kings (*Edwards*) 8.99
The Prisoner in the Third Cell (*Edwards*) 7.99
Letters to a Devastated Christian (*Edwards*) 7.95
Exquisite Agony *(Edwards)* 8.95
Dear Lillian (*Edwards*) *paperback* 5.95
Dear Lillian *(Edwards) hardcover* 9.99

OTHER BOOKS ON CHURCH LIFE

Climb the Highest Mountain (*Edwards*) 12.95
The Torch of the Testimony (*Kennedy*) 14.95
The Passing of the Torch (*Chen*) 9.95
Going to Church in the First Century (*Banks*) 5.95
When the Church was Young (*Loosley*) 8.95
Church Unity *(Litzman,Nee,Edwards)* 10.95
Let's Return to Christian Unity *(Kurosaki)* 10.95
Rethinking the Wineskin *(Viola)* 9.95
Who is Your Covering? *(Viola)* 7.95

CHRISTIAN LIVING

The Autobiography of Jeanne Guyon 19.95
Final Steps in Christian Maturity (*Guyon*) 12.95
Turkeys and Eagles (*Lord*) 8.95
The Life of Jeanne Guyon *(T.C. Upham)* 17.95
Life's Ultimate Privilege (*Fromke*) 10.00
Unto Full Stature (*Fromke*) 10.00
All and Only (*Kilpatrick*) 7.95
Adoration (*Kilpatrick*) 8.95
Release of the Spirit (*Nee*) 9.99
Bone of His Bone (*Huegel*) *modernized* 8.95

Prices subject to change